Making Money

Abby Jackson
AR B.L.: 2.0
Points: 0.5   LG

Yellow Umbrella Books are published by Capstone Press
151 Good Counsel Drive, P.O. Box 669, Mankato, Minnesota 56002
www.capstonepress.com

Library of Congress Cataloging-in-Publication Data
Jackson, Abby.
    Making money / by Abby Jackson.
    p. cm.
    Summary: Simple text and photographs introduce the purpose of money, how old
coins and paper money are disposed of, and how new money is made.
    ISBN 0-7368-2928-8 (hardcover)—ISBN 0-7368-2887-7 (softcover)
    1. Money—Juvenile literature. 2. Money—United States—Juvenile literature.
[1. Money.] I. Title.
HG221.5.J33 2004
332.4—dc21   2003010971

Editorial Credits
Editorial Director: Mary Lindeen
Editor: Jennifer VanVoorst
Photo Researcher: Wanda Winch
Developer: Raindrop Publishing

Photo Credits
Cover: PhotoLink/Photodisc; Title Page: DigitalVision; Page 2: PhotoLink/Photodisc;
Page 3: Russell Illig/Photodisc; Page 4: Richard Harris/Index Stock Imagery; Page 5:
Rim Light/PhotoLink/Photodisc; Page 6: Ryan McVay/Photodisc; Page 7: Ed Castle/
Folio, Inc.; Page 8: PhotoLink/Photodisc; Page 9: James Leynse/Corbis Saba; Page 10:
DigitalVision; Page 11: Bureau of Engraving and Printing/Department of the U.S.
Treasury; Page 12: Bruce Leighty/The Image Finders; Page 13: Photo courtesy of the
U.S. Mint; Page 14: Photo courtesy of the U.S. Mint; Page 15: Photo courtesy of the U.S.
Mint; Page 16: Ryan McVay/Photodisc

1 2 3 4 5 6 09 08 07 06 05 04

Making Money

by Abby Jackson

Consultant: Dwight Herold, EdD, Past President,
Iowa Council for the Social Studies

Yellow Umbrella Books

an imprint of Capstone Press
Mankato, Minnesota

We Need Money

There are things that we need
in order to live. There are also
things that we want.

Most of these things are not free. We must pay money for them.

Food and clothing cost money.
Toys cost money. Even a bus
ride is not free.

People work at jobs to earn money. Sometimes they save their money. Other times they use their money to buy things.

Old Money

Money gets passed from person to person. Sometimes money gets old and worn out.

What happens to money that is too old to use? Big machines tear paper money into tiny pieces.

THIS PACKAGE CONTAINS
SHREDDINGS OF

150

IN GENUINE
UNITED STATES CURRENCY
PRINTED AT THE
BUREAU OF ENGRAVING AND PRINTING
WASHINGTON, D.C.

Coins last longer than
paper money. It is rare
to get a very old coin.

The government makes new
money to replace the old money.

Making Money

What we call paper money is not really made from paper. It is made from cotton and linen.

Paper money is printed at a special place. When the bills are ready, they are delivered to banks.

Coins are made at a different
place. A place that makes coins
is called a mint.

Coins start as big sheets of metal. Then small circles are punched out of the metal.

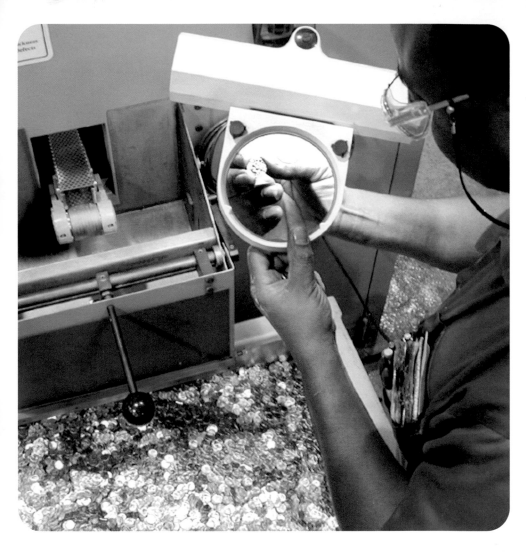

Words and pictures are stamped into the coins. Workers check the coins for mistakes.

The coins are put into big bags. The bags are taken to the bank.

The money goes from the bank to you! What do you do with your money?

Words to Know/Index

Word Count: 234
Early-Intervention Level: 16